Marriage Is...

A Marriage Enrichment

21-Day Devotional

M. ANN WEST

CONTENT

DEDICATION

ACKNOWLEDGMENTS

FOREWORD

INTRODUCTION

DEDICATION

Lord, I want to thank You because without You I am nothing, but with You I can do all things.

This book is dedicated to the love of my life, Wink West. You have inspired me, encouraged me, and have been my greatest supporter. We can't do life alone, and I am blessed to have you as my life partner. Thank you for all you do in our marriage, and for showing me what Marriage Is!

I love you. *#mybestfriend*

M. ANN WEST

ACKNOWLEDGMENTS

I have been so blessed to have amazing people in my life who have supported me. My dad and mom, William "Billy" and Celia Boyd, for giving me life and supporting everything I have ever done. My two most favorite handsome sons, Shawn and Sherrod, I love being your mom and I hope you make fine husbands for two fortunate women, like your dad has been to me. William Jr. "Phee," my one and only brother, I have been praying for you for a long time, and you are a big part of why I pray every day. I love you brother! **#family1st**

A special thanks to Pastors Alex and Tammy Rivera for seeing what God saw in Wink and me. You both gave us the opportunity to pour into so many couples through the Marriage Enrichment Ministry over the last few years. To our Journey Church family, we want to thank you for being you. We appreciate you all, for without you this devotional would not have been birthed.

To Mr. Norman and Bertha Morgan, thank you for giving Wink and me so much love, support, and advice over the years. Your guidance contributed immensely to our marriage journey. You Rock! **#mentors4life**

FOREWORD

There are very few people of this generation who are qualified to speak biblically and practically on the subject of marriage. Without question, one of those voices is Ann West. I have had the privilege of gleaning from the wisdom that Ann and her husband Wink possess on this topic. Their commitment to God's Word, and being authentic, have been a tremendous blessing to so many in the body of Christ.

In this 21-Day Devotional, Ann takes the reader on a journey through God's heart for marriage. Each day is filled with strong biblical content and a guide for practical application. The reader will be engaged with creative illustrations, and clear instructions, on how to apply what they have learned.

Please don't wait another moment. Dive into this devotional heart first and you'll be amazed at the change you will experience.

—**Alex Rivera**
Lead Pastor
Journey Church

M. ANN WEST

INTRODUCTION

It's Not About You!

For many years I have been privileged to share with single women, women who are engaged, and married couples the struggles that come with marriage. The one fact that continues to resonate is that the relationship is not just about you; the two become one, and you must die to self and give 100% to the relationship. When you say, "I do," there is no manual of instructions—marriage is full blown on the job training. It has been God's grace and mercy that has allowed us to get where we are now. I often say, "If I knew then what I know now, we could have avoided so many bumps in the road."

God sustained, and healed our relationship, and for that I am grateful. He kept us married! I love the man that God gave me. I appreciate our struggle and how it has helped us become who we are today.

When I look back over the past 36 years all I can say is, "Thank you, Lord, for keeping us."

My prayer is that you will be able to check your heart and

have an unclouded vision of what marriage really is. Learn to enjoy your relationship, put God first, be honest with yourself, and know that you are in it for an eternity. Embrace the journey!

Marriage is the most sacred relationship that gives the world a picture of God's love toward us. There is no blueprint, book for dummies, or a "how to in 30 days" that can give this covenant relationship a clear snapshot of what life in marriage is all about.

My husband and I recently attended a 60th wedding anniversary party. It was amazing to see this handsome couple, who have been battle tested, show what the power of God and marriage covenant can do.

Their story isn't a fairytale. It is wrapped in the death of loved ones, sickness neigh unto death, deterioration, loss of limbs, and life itself. The two of them, happy as can be, were sitting at their diamond anniversary round table.

I wonder, God, what is the secret? What would keep two people together in a marriage literally full of battle scars, physical ailments early in their relationship, tears, heartache, and situations that would cause you to quit? What kept their union of a lifetime together? The Scripture that comes to mind is this: *"Let this mind be in you, which was also in Christ Jesus"* (Philippians 2:5). In the NIV

(New International Version), it says, "In your relationships with one another, have the same mindset as Christ Jesus."

This tells me that this couple was intentional about their relationship with God and with one another. I know that their journey didn't begin this way, but God had chosen their path and He knew the road that would be taken and the end result. Many may ask the questions: What is marriage? What keeps a marriage together? What is marriage in the eyes of God? As you begin this journey of reflection in your marriage, be intentional. Allow the Lord to speak to your heart and be purposeful about what God requires of you. Let's begin.

What is your goal in your marriage?

_____

_____

_____

_____

_____

_____

_____

What do you pray for in your marriage?

_____

_____

_____

_____

_____

_____

_____

DAY 1

MARRIAGE IS COMMITMENT

You must have the mindset that you are going to do it God's way. Oftentimes after reciting our vows, we really don't realize that it's a commitment made before man and God. Today, most couples do not experience the longevity that their parents and grandparents have had. In the 21st century, it is becoming a foreign concept. If a couple celebrates 20 years of being together, it is seen as a lifetime. Marriage is not sacred to them. The makeup of what marriage looks like today is far from what was originally intended. Today, we have names for marriages such as Hollywood, common law, same sex, etc. But God intended for there to be one type of marriage—a covenant relationship between one man and one woman (Genesis 2:24).

Marriage is a covenant, an agreement, a coming together, a treaty, an alliance, a promise between two parties, God and man. In our sinful desires, we have shaped marriage to be what we want, not what God ordained.

Marriage is more than just having sex.

Marriage is more than just having a roommate.

Marriage is more than just saving our finances.

Marriage is more than just having children.

Marriage is so much more.

I am amazed at the pictures we have painted of this covenant relationship. Through social media, radio, and television the face of marriage has changed. In our culture today, marriage has become about our feelings: How long can you make me happy? How long can I love you and all of your imperfections, those that I see and those that have yet to be revealed? Can we do this? Do I really want to do this?

Numbers 30:1–2 says, *"This is what the LORD commands: When a man makes a vow to the LORD or takes an oath to obligate himself by a pledge, he must not break his word but must do everything he said"* (NIV). This is the commitment that we make to one another. It is our responsibility to honor our commitment. Jesus Christ honored His commitment to us on Calvary's cross. Let's do the same. Honor your commitment.

Aspiration: What is your commitment in your marriage

and the vows you made?

_____

_____

_____

_____

_____

_____

Prayer: What is your prayer for the commitment you made?

_____

_____

_____

_____

_____

_____

_____

M. ANN WEST

DAY 2

MARRIAGE IS FOUNDATIONAL

It is how life begins for male and female, believers in Christ. It is fundamental. You read about the first marriage in the book of Genesis between Adam and Eve. Yet, today marriage has been reduced to a concept that some agree to while others opt out of. The notion of two people beginning a life together with a true commitment is considered passé. You don't think about you and your spouse being the foundation of a lifelong relationship. Marriage is the starting point of a partnership with two people coming together with distinct ideals, different practices, and diverse attitudes on how the relationship will work.

They merge into ideals that become foundational for their relationship with one another. In the book of Genesis, once God created Adam, He put him to sleep and created Eve from his rib as a helpmate (Genesis 2:18, 21-22). This was their beginning. This is how it all started. Your foundation begins when you say I do! This is your groundwork for becoming one with another person. We take and make the vow, but so often its sincerity is not a reality. It is just a mere formality. We look forward to the wedding ceremony, the friends in attendance, the venue so lovely decorated, the party that lasts all night, and the honeymoon; a trip to an exotic island for two. We see, hear, and feel the romance of it all. But what about the covenant? What about the institution of this joining together? Rereading my own wedding vows remind me of how our journey began.

This is the traditional vow that many people recite unless they create their own.

"I _____ take you to be my lawfully wedded (husband or wife) to have and to hold, from this day forward, for better, for worse, for richer, for poorer, in sickness and in health, until death do us part."

This vow became the foundation of our life together and the promise that was made to one another. Is this the promise you espoused to?

Mark 10:6-9 says, *"But at the beginning of creation God made them male and female. For this reason a man shall leave his father and mother and be united to his wife, and the two will become one flesh. So they are no longer two, but one flesh. Therefore what God has joined together let no one separate"* (NIV).

This is the foundation of your relationship. Keep your foundation stable and watch God build upon it! Honor your vow!

Aspiration: Looking back at the vows you took on your wedding day, how committed are you to what you professed?

_____

_____

_____

_____

_____

_____

_____

Prayer: What are you asking God to do with the vow you made on your wedding day?

_____

_____

_____

_____

_____

DAY 3

MARRIAGE IS SACRIFICIAL

You don't think of marriage in those terms, but that is the reality of the relationship. Typically, we don't get married with the intention of giving anything up. Rather, the intention is to gain some things. Normally, you gain a new last name as the wife. You gain wealth with your combined incomes. You gain the privilege of becoming parents. You gain stability and companionship with one another. So, where does the sacrifice come into play? And beyond that, why should you have to sacrifice? You didn't get married to make sacrifices, did you? You got married to be happy, to feel loved, to be taken care of, to have someone to talk and to snuggle up with at night. Sacrifice, really? In our 36 years of marriage, I have had to make some sacrifices not only for myself, but for my husband as well. Did it always feel good? No! Did it always make sense? No! Was it the right thing to do? Yes! When I made it not about me, I became a sacrificial person.

Here are some things to remember:

Marriage is a give and take.

Marriage is a balancing act.

Marriage is a selfless decision.

Marriage is a way to stay close to God.

Marriage is a reason to stay at the feet of Jesus.

Marriage is an experience of a lifetime.

A marriage made easy can only come from God. We must follow His plan and direction as He orders our steps. Ephesians 5:2 says, *"And walk in the way of love, just as Christ loved us and gave himself up for us as a fragrant offering and sacrifice to God"* (ESV). The greatest sacrifice was made to us by God. Jesus died on the cross for our sins. Can the sacrifice you make in your marriage compare?

Aspiration: What sacrifices do you want to make to please God and your spouse?

_____

_____

_____

_____

_____

_____

_____

Prayer: Lord, help me to become more sacrificial in my relationship with my spouse. (Be specific about the change(s) you want to make).

_____

_____

_____

_____

_____

_____

_____

DAY 4

MARRIAGE IS A CORNERSTONE

Marriage reflects God's relationship between Him as our father and us as His bride. A cornerstone is the first stone that a mason sets in the foundation of a building. The cornerstone itself is a ceremonial stone that is set in a prominent location on the outside of the building. It usually has an inscription of the date or year it was constructed and the names of the architect and builder. Our marriages were constructed by God on the date we vowed to follow His commands. He is the architect that has designed our relationship with one another. He is the foundation upon which our marriage is to be built. Yes, we are the cornerstone. We are the beginning of something new. Everyday becomes a day of thanksgiving for what the builder—Christ—built.

We were constructed to be the helpmate for one another. There is no replication of our marriage. We are all originals. We may have similar circumstances, but they have been tailor-made especially for us. Every building—marriage—represents God in a specific way, but the ultimate plan of the builder is to bring glory and honor to Himself.

Isaiah 28:16 says, *"Therefore, the Lord God said, Look, I have laid a stone in Zion, a tested stone, a precious cornerstone, a sure foundation, the one who believes will be unshakeable"* (HCSB).

You are precious to God. And when you build your marriage on the firm foundation of Him and His Word, you will be unshakeable. You will become a force to be reckoned with. You will bend, but not break. You will falter, but you won't fail. You will become victorious in your relationship.

Aspiration: How can you create a foundation that will be the cornerstone of your relationship?

_____

_____

_____

_____

_____

_____

_____

Prayer: What prayer of commitment can you make to God as it relates to your marriage being a cornerstone?

_____

_____

_____

_____

_____

_____

DAY 5

MARRIAGE IS ABOUT BECOMING

It will take you a lifetime to become what God wants you to be. You have to be battle tested by the experiences of weathering a few storms. Marriage, done God's way, means making a decision to honor the blueprint you were given. In order to become one with your mate, you have to die to yourself and allow God to mold and reshape you. Nothing just is! Things are created and designed by the master builder. When I said I do, I thought I was everything that I needed to be. I thought I came with all the ingredients to create this wonderful life and marriage. No, changes were necessary. To my surprise, there wasn't much of me that was usable in creating this marriage masterpiece. God began to show me there were fragments that could be placed in one area of the masterpiece.

However, there were many pieces that were broken, but could be repaired, and recycled. Thanks be to the glory of God for His masterful plan. He knew what I needed to become all that He wanted me to be. There's good news! God has that same plan for you and your spouse. It's amazing how we often see ourselves as all that before marriage. Then suddenly after marriage, we find ourselves in a power struggle with our mates. I want what I want and he or she wants what he or she wants. The question becomes: What does God want? What should my marriage look like to Him? How does He want my life and marriage to show His glory? He wants you to become one with the person to whom you have committed your life.

God wants you to become a three-cord strand: you, your spouse, and God in the center. This is a knot that is not easily unraveled. With that combination, you will always succeed. There is no way the strands can become untied or separated. Ecclesiastes 4:12 says, *"Though one may be overpowered, two can defend themselves. A cord of three strands is not quickly broken"* (NIV). A three-cord strand is not easily broken. It is extremely difficult to unravel. When God is the third cord, Satan can't break what was joined together by God.

Aspiration: How do you see yourself becoming one with your spouse?

_____

_____

_____

_____

_____

_____

Prayer: What prayer of commitment can you make to God as it relates to becoming one?

_____

_____

_____

_____

_____

_____

DAY 6

MARRIAGE IS FRUITFUL

God through the Holy Spirit has produced in you and your spouse fruit to be used for His glory. In marriage and for a bountiful life, you should exemplify all of the characteristics found in Galatians 5:22-23. There are times when you become so complacent with the one you have pledged your affections to, that you forget that these characteristics should always remain in the marriage. You must be purposeful when you are developing the fruit of the Spirit. A daily dose of consistency and intentionally checking your emotions is essential. When emotions are out of control, our marriages are out of control. Developing the fruit of the Spirit is very beneficial. It lays the ground work for effective communication.

It brings peace to the household, while drawing you closer to God.

Galatians 5:22-23 says, *"But the Holy Spirit produces*

this kind of fruit in our lives: love, joy [gladness of heart], peace, patience [having an even temper], kindness [excellence in character], goodness [being good towards others], faithfulness, gentleness [having no self-interest], and self-control. There is no law against these things" (NLT).

When you respond using the fruit of the Spirit, your outcome will always be positive. The fruit of the Spirit is foundational for your life in Christ. Your actions and demeanor depend on how you manifest the fruit in your life. Everything that you say and do is directly related to the fruit of the Spirit.

Aspiration: Do you work on the fruit of the Spirit daily? Where do you need more growth?

_____

_____

_____

_____

_____

_____

Prayer: Lord, help me with my ... (be specific about the fruit of the Spirit that you need to incorporate more of in your life, especially how it relates to your spouse).

_____

_____

_____

_____

_____

_____

DAY 7

MARRIAGE IS WORK

Marriage is the one thing that doesn't come with a "how to" manual. It is all on the job training. It doesn't matter how many pre-marital counseling sessions you receive (and believe me it is very important to have premarital counseling), it is work, a job, a career. You are constantly learning new skills every day. Just when you think you have mastered an area, a new one comes along. You will put in a lot of effort and exertion in your relationship with your spouse. You will feel tired and spent on many days, but other days you will wonder why isn't everyday just like the one you are experiencing. There is no retirement package in marriage. It is a lifelong commitment until the Lord takes you home to be with Him.

You must be able to handle and resolve conflict. You must be able to tell the truth in love. You must be able to put your spouse's feelings before yours. You must be able to think outside the box. You must be able to create an atmosphere of reassurance. Your spouse must be able to trust you and know that you have his or her best interest in mind. You have to be able to wear many hats and sometimes a few at the same time. You must make marriage a priority. I know that for some time I didn't take my marriage seriously. It caused much anxiety on the part of my spouse and me. Again, you must be intentional about the investment that you make. Just like you receive an evaluation on your job, God is constantly evaluating your relationship with your spouse. Remember he or she is looking for a reflection. God already knows what will give you an outstanding or exceptional rating. At the end of this life, He will say, *"Well done thy good and faithful servant"* (Matthew 25:23).

1 Corinthians 15:58 says, *"So, my dear brothers and sisters, be strong and immovable. Always work enthusiastically for the Lord, for you know that nothing you do for the Lord is ever useless"* (NLT).

Nothing you do for Christ will go unnoticed. He has equipped you to work and produce a great harvest with your spouse. Keep your hand to the plow and don't look back. Keep allowing God to create in you that passion for the work and effort that you put into your marriage. You will reap the benefits.

Aspiration: Do you feel that you are putting a 100% work ethic into your marriage? If so, explain. If not, then why not?

_____

_____

_____

_____

_____

_____

_____

Prayer: Looking at the time and energy you spend working on your marriage, what improvements can you ask the Lord to help you with?

_____

_____

_____

_____

_____

_____

_____

M. ANN WEST

DAY 8

MARRIAGE IS NOT ABOUT YOU

How many times have you made your marriage about you? It is very easy to do so, because when you get married you are looking at the gains and pluses of the relationship—not the giving and taking away.

You have questions that you ask yourself, but you would never dare verbalize, because you don't want to be seen as selfish. What do you hope to gain? Marriage is about Christ; you just get to experience some of the perks along the way. Everything created on earth has a purpose; it is to show the manifest presence of God. You were created to show the manifest presence of God. Your spouse was created to show the manifest presence of God. Your marriage was created to show the manifest presence of God.

In the counseling sessions, we hear these phrases:

I don't feel loved.

I don't feel heard.

45

I don't feel understood.

I don't feel respected.

I don't feel honored.

I don't feel_____ you fill in the blank. Have you taken a moment to ask God the same question? Lord do you know/feel that I love you, hear you, understand you, respect you, honor you, etc.? Wow! What you are expecting from your spouse you haven't given to God—the one who created you! Are you expecting more than you are willing to give?

Revelation 4:11 says, "*You are worthy, O Lord our God, to receive glory and honor and power. For you created all things, and they exist because you created what pleased you*" (NIV).

Do you have realistic and unrealistic expectations of your spouse? Is the pot calling the kettle black? Are you making your marriage about you and not about the one who created you?

Aspiration: Have you in times past made your marriage about you? Is there anything you need to apologize to your spouse about, because you made it about you?

_____

_____

_____

_____

_____

_____

_____

Prayer: Write a prayer of repentance for making situations about yourself.

_____

_____

_____

_____

_____

_____

_____

M. ANN WEST

DAY 9

MARRIAGE IS CULTIVATION

Every marriage needs cultivation, which is improvement on growth. If you are not growing and developing in your marriage you will be malnourished, which could lead to death. Just as your physical body needs nourishment and air, so does your marriage. It is highly unlikely that a plant would survive without some care. A plant requires water, air, sunlight, and nutrients. Those same ingredients are required in your marriage. Water is what keeps your marriage replenished. You need the watering or washing of the Word of God to stay planted, to grow, and to build deep roots. In marriage, you want to be rooted and grounded so that you can stand the test of time. You also need sunlight to grow.

In your relationship with one another, there is always a growth spurt. The energy from the Son of God is our light.

As you walk in the light of God's Word, it will keep you healthy, whole, and strong.

Nutrients, which are required daily, are found in your obedience to the Word of God. As you continue to become fit in your marriage and build up stamina, you are able to praise the Lord and give thanks to Him for His marvelous greatness. Marriage requires air too. Jesus is the air that you breathe. He continues to breathe life into your life day by day.

2 Peter 3:18 says, *"But grow in the grace and knowledge of our Lord and Savior Jesus Christ. To him be glory, both now and to the day of eternity. Amen"* (NASB). As you cultivate your marriage, you bring fullness to your relationship with your spouse and our Savior.

Aspiration: How do you plan to cultivate your marriage?

_____

_____

_____

_____

_____

_____

Prayer: The Lord requires us to grow. What are you willing to pray about concerning the cultivation of your marriage?

_____

_____

MARRIAGE IS...

_____

_____

_____

_____

_____

DAY 10

MARRIAGE IS GRATITUDE

Gratitude should be a mainstay in your relationship. Are you grateful every day for having someone with whom you share your life? Do you appreciate having someone that you can grow old with, someone who loves you for who you are, and someone who can help you become all that God has intended you to be? Some of the many joys of marriage include having a personal cheerleader, mentor, friend, and so much more. There is always a reason to be grateful. Having someone to share those moments with are priceless. To experience a tragedy and triumph with the love of your life is a reason to be grateful. There are countless people in the world who would love to have someone to whom they come home. They would love to have a partner that would hold them accountable in life. Together we have so much to be grateful for, our salvation is the biggest gift of gratitude that we share. Thank you, Jesus.

1 Thessalonians 5:18 says, "In everything give thanks: for this is the will of God in Christ Jesus concerning you." There will always be a reason to be grateful to God for the sacrifice He made on your behalf. He allowed His only Son to die on the cross so that you may live. Let's show Him we are grateful, give Him PRAISE!!

Aspiration: Do you think you give God enough thanks for all that He has done for you, your spouse, and your marriage?

_____

_____

_____

_____

_____

_____

_____

Prayer: This is a time when you can give God a prayer of gratitude for all that He has done for you.

_____

_____

_____

_____

_____

_____

_____

M. ANN WEST

DAY 11

MARRIAGE IS PURPOSEFUL

Every marriage has a purpose. There are always reasons why God put two people together. In your perspective, you may think it is about the love you have for one another. That does not compare to what God had in mind when He designed marriage. The purpose is always bigger than you could imagine.

Marriage was instituted for family.

Marriage was instituted for provision.

Marriage was instituted for fellowship.

Marriage was instituted for companionship.

Marriage was instituted for population and protection from sexual immorality.

Marriage was instituted for Christ and the church.

Marriage is God's institution for showing an unselfish love. This relationship is a reflection to the church of Christ's unfailing love. Christ gave His life for His bride, which is the church. In His selfless act, He provides an example of how a husband should treat his wife. Our marriages are a foretaste of things to come. When Christ comes back for His bride, the church, there will be a ceremony uniting us back with Him (Revelation 19:7-9; 21:1-2)

When God created marriage, He had us in mind. Adam and Eve were the first couple. He entrusted the earth to them and gave them instructions on how to manage on the earth. Just as His love for us has been demonstrated, we are to do the same for one another.

Genesis 2:18 says, *"Then the Lord God said, It is not good that the man should be alone; I will make him a helper fit for him" (ESV).*

Genesis 2:23-24 says, "At last! the man exclaimed. This one is bone from my bone, and flesh from my flesh! She will be called woman, because she was taken from man. This explains why a man leaves his father and mother and is joined to his wife, and the two are united into one" (NLT).

Marriage is a powerful institution with the master designer and His gracious love for humanity. Indeed, "Marriage is meant by God to put the Gospel reality on display in the world."

Aspiration: Do you see the purpose for which God has brought you and your spouse together? What do you think is the reason?

_____

_____

_____

_____

_____

_____

_____

Prayer: The purpose for your marriage is ordained by God. What prayer can you offer him concerning you and your spouse?

_____

_____

_____

_____

_____

_____

John Piper, This Momentary Marriage: A Parable Of Permanence, (Wheaton: Crossways, 2009), 26.

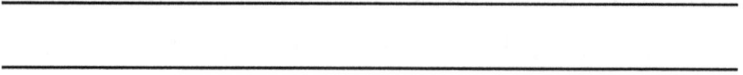

DAY 12

MARRIAGE IS FORGIVING

Forgiveness is a mandate in marriage. This can be seen as one of the hardest challenges to conquer. Your relationship will not survive without it. Forgiveness is considered hard when you feel that you have been wronged. The sting and pain of the hurt linger and stick to you like a band-aid on your skin. The adhesive attached to you becomes painful when you remove it. Forgiveness is removing the band-aid. It is allowing the hurt to be exposed so that it can heal properly. When you forgive, you heal. The sting of the hurt no longer binds you. You become free. Forgiveness is a daily practice. When you don't forgive, you become spiritually depleted which can result in other sicknesses that can deprive you of a healthy marriage. Lack of forgiveness creates pride, bitterness, selfishness and so many other negative emotions.

When you forgive, it brings healing to your physical body

and mental state of mind.

When you forgive, it shows the power of God's love.

When you forgive, it shows the world the unfailing power of God's grace.

When you forgive, it shows the power of the cross.

When you forgive, it shows freedom from Satan's attempted attacks.

When you forgive, heaven's gates are open.

When you forgive, it shows love and obedience to the Word of God.

In marriage, it seems that forgiveness becomes a struggle. You will forgive a stranger sooner than you would your spouse. Why is that? Is the expectation greater? Do you hold your spouse hostage to an unrealistic expectation? Is there an action that you find unforgivable? Is there ever an offense that can't be forgiven?

Matthew 18:21-22 says, *Then Peter came up and said to him, "Lord, how often will my brother sin against me, and I forgive him? As many as seven times?"*

Jesus said to him, "I do not say to you seven times, but seventy times seven" (ESV).

Aspiration: Have you exercised your forgiveness tank for the day? Is it easy for you to forgive your spouse? Or do you need a new strategy?

_____

_____

_____

_____

_____

_____

_____

Prayer: The lack of forgiveness is too heavy for you to bear alone. What do you need to ask God in terms of your level of forgiveness?

_____

_____

_____

_____

_____

_____

_____

M. ANN WEST

DAY 13

MARRIAGE IS HONESTY

Honesty is the best policy. It is often said, we want honesty. But at what price are you willing to give your honest opinion? And at what price are you willing to receive an honest opinion? One thing we all know is that truth sometimes hurts. In marriage, no one intentionally wants to hurt the other person, but it happens. When honesty knocks, it sometimes changes your attitude. You become humiliated and frustrated, or you become the super hero to save the day. The Word of God commands us to speak the truth in love. So, honesty has a wrapper on it. It has a covering on it. It has been dipped in love so that pain, hurt, or anxiety doesn't rear its ugly head. In marriage, you have to share ugly truths, but not so ugly that you intentionally hurt the other person. Presentation is everything. True honesty means feeling comfortable enough to share with our mate what is seen and said. Out of the abundance of the heart, the mouth speaks. Is your heart right? Do you need a heart check before you speak? Jesus has always shown examples throughout the Bible where He was brutally honest with the people, but He loved them up at the same time. You are today's earthly example of honesty. You are the vehicle being used to share the truth with your spouse, because the truth makes you stronger and wiser! In all situations and conversations, our goal should be speaking honestly, covered in the love of Christ.

When you are honest with your spouse, your love for one another will grow.

When you are honest with your spouse, you create a safe place to be vulnerable.

When you are honest with your spouse, your relationship with God will become stronger.

When you are honest with your spouse, you become honest with God.

Proverbs 12:17 says, *"He who speaks truth tells what is right, But a false witness, deceit"* (NASB)

Ephesians 4:15-16 says, *"Instead, we will speak the truth in love, growing in every way more and more like Christ, who is the head of his body, the church. He makes the whole body fit together perfectly. As each part does its own special work, it helps the other parts grow, so that the whole body is healthy and growing and full of love"* (NLT). Your goal should be to look like Jesus. To think what would Jesus do, and more than that, what would Jesus say!

Aspiration: Lord, I want to be honest in my conversations with my spouse. Write down what you will need to do to make that happen.

_____

_____

_____

_____

_____

_____

_____

Prayer: I want to speak the truth in love to my spouse at all times. My prayer is:

_____

_____

_____

_____

_____

_____

M. ANN WEST

DAY 14

MARRIAGE IS JOY

Joy is the emotion of happiness caused by something pleasurable. The joy of the Lord is your strength. You are strengthened when you have joy. As life transcends your relationship with one another, you will experience some highs and lows and with that comes an assault on your contentment. Do you know how to be content? Do you know how to sustain your joy in the midst of a crisis? When things go awry, or you feel like you've reached the end of your rope with your mate, is your joy sustainable? It is all about perspective. Your outlook will have an effect on your experiences with your mate. Remember, building your spiritual muscles is all part of the journey. When life becomes a whirlwind, you have to lean in to one another, not away from one another. You are strengthened when you experience God's joy.

Circumstances may intervene, but the joy of the Lord still has a hold on you. Job experienced much calamity in his life. He was a righteous man who loved God. His life seemed to spiral out of control, yet he still held on to the Lord. During his journey, Job allowed God to build his spiritual muscles. True joy comes from Christ and not our circumstances. Joy is that life jacket that keeps you afloat until the rescue boat saves you.

John 15:11 says, *"I have spoken these things to you so that my joy may be in you and your joy may be complete"* (HCSB).

Joy is that inner peace that can't be explained and all you can say is "no worries!" It is the part of you that makes you put your hands in the air and cry out!

I have found my joy!

I declare my joy!

I receive my joy!

I thank you for my joy!

Aspiration: Do you encourage your spouse to keep the joy of the Lord when times seem difficult? What do you do or say?

_____

_____

_____

_____

_____

_____

_____

Prayer: What is your prayer to God for handling difficult circumstances?

_____

_____

_____

_____

_____

_____

M. ANN WEST

DAY 15

MARRIAGE IS RESPECT

There is a popular gospel song entitled "Worth" sung by Anthony Brown. This song grips your heart and makes you so thankful to God. The Lord thought that you were worth salvation, and that He thought enough of you to die on the cross. Respect is having esteem or the sense of a person's worth. You came into this world with worth. No matter how sinful or filthy your life may be, Christ thought it was worth saving. When you married your spouse, in essence you were saying that they were worth something to you. He or she was worth your time, your attention, and your care. In the book of Ephesians, wives are commanded to respect their husbands and husbands are commanded to love their wives as they love themselves (Ephesians 5:33). When husbands and wives have self-respect, they can readily show respect to one another. The world tells us that respect must be earned; it's something that both young and old are seeking to find and receive. How do you earn a person's respect? How do you earn your spouse's respect?

You earn your spouse's respect by:

Safeguarding their dignity,

Safeguarding their values,

Safeguarding who they are,

Safeguarding their heart,

Safeguarding their commitment,

Safeguarding their love,

And safeguarding their worth.

1 Peter 3:14-16 says, *"But even if you should suffer for righteousness sake, you will be blessed. Have no fear of them, nor be troubled, but in your hearts honor Christ the Lord as holy, always being prepared to make a defense to anyone who asks you for a reason for the hope that is in you; yet do it with gentleness and respect, having a good conscience, so that, when you are slandered, those who revile your good behavior in Christ may be put to shame"* (ESV).

Respect is a two-way street. It brings joy to the life of the other person. When you are respected, it gives you pep in your step. It allows you to feel important. It gives you strength and encouragement.

Aspiration: How do you show your spouse respect? Do you give him or her what they need?

_____

_____

_____

_____

_____

_____

_____

Prayer: Everyone needs to be respected. Ask the Lord to show you how to respect your spouse more in the areas where they need it.

_____

_____

_____

_____

_____

_____

_____

M. ANN WEST

DAY 16

MARRIAGE IS HONOR

Honoring a person is showing that you have high regard for them. Examples of people who have earned honor include the President of the United States, the CEO of a corporation and the Queen of England, just to name a few. These people have a place of status, they are powerful. They make important decisions on behalf of others. You value their opinion. You esteem them. And if you were in their presence, you would treat them with great respect. It is amazing how we have such high regard for people that we don't know. Now think about this, you have a companion who has pledged his or her love and devotion to you, yet he or she has frequently been shown "no honor." They are sometimes treated like a roommate, or someone you just like hanging out with on occasion.

Knowingly or unknowingly, you may be treating them in a

disrespectful manner. This could leave your mate feeling like he or she is being taken advantage of. Is that you? Instead of being dishonoring, you should honor your mate as someone who is created in God's image. God blesses us for how we treat our mate. Others are watching you. Your children are watching you. Your friends are watching you. God is watching you! He's looking at how you treat His child. How you treat that person that He created just for you, the gift that He gave you.

Just like a child that insists on having his/her own way; they badger their parents until they get the desired object; once they get it, it no longer has the value that once was attached to it. It loses its importance. This can often happen in marriages. You've got to have your spouse. You have been watching them, thinking about them, praying for them, but once you get them, they are tossed aside like yesterday's news. When you honor your spouse, you honor God. You are humbled and think more highly of him or her than yourself. When you honor your spouse, you value them, you esteem them, and you treat them with great respect. The same regard that you have for the President, CEO, and the Queen should be of greater value for your spouse.

Romans 12:10 says, *"Love each other with genuine*

affection, and take delight in honoring each other" (NLT).
The Bible instructs us to honor one another, in doing so we
please God.

Aspiration: In honoring your spouse, how will it benefit
your relationship?

_____

_____

_____

_____

_____

_____

_____

Prayer: The Bible says to take delight in honoring each
other. What would you like to pray for as it relates to
honoring your spouse?

_____

_____

_____

_____

_____

_____

M. ANN WEST

DAY 17

MARRIAGE IS SECURITY

Everyone wants to feel safe and secure. It is important in marriage that you protect your spouse's heart and feelings. When you give your heart to someone, you expose yourself to them. You hope that as you expose yourself that there is someone to cover you. You put your feelings out there trusting that the other person realizes how precious this part of you is. It is very important that you protect one another's heart. When you say "I do," you are in essence saying "I trust that you will protect me." It is important that you don't let each other's heart be unsecured. When things are left unsecured, they are stolen. You don't want anyone to steal the best part of you. Your devotion for one another and the feeling of being safe gives you a sense of relief. Your relationship with your spouse is the glue that will sustain you in times of uncertainty. When you make your spouse feel secure, it opens up opportunities to grow deeper. This gives purpose to your life and it gives you comfort knowing that you are protected.

Everyone becomes vulnerable at one time or another in the relationship. It is good to know that your spouse is that person who is protecting you. Think of this in terms of our heavenly Father. He is your security and your protector. The Holy Spirit was given to you as a comforter. The Holy Spirit guards your heart and mind. You feel secure in knowing that He is watching over you, like a security guard. Your spouse is your security guard. His or her presence should bring you the feeling of being emotionally secure. You both should feel secure about the love that you have for one another. Your security gives you the confidence in knowing that you can weather any storm together. You feel secure in knowing that someone is praying for you always, that someone is building you up, and that someone is walking on the same path as you. You feel secure in knowing that Christ is the center of his or her life as well.

Hebrews 13:5b-6 says, *"For He Himself has said, I will never leave you nor forsake you. So we may boldly say: The LORD is my helper; I will not fear. What can man do to me?"* (NKJV).

Psalm 91:1-4 says, *"Whoever dwells in the shelter of the*

Most High will rest in the shadow of the Almighty. I will say of the Lord, He is my refuge and my fortress, my God, in whom I trust. Surely he will save you from the fowler's snare and from the deadly pestilence. He will cover you with his feathers, and under his wings you will find refuge; his faithfulness will be your shield and rampart" (NIV).

In your marriage, it is important that the two of you are secure in your relationship with one another. Be secure with your relationship with Christ. Remember only what you do for Christ will last.

Aspiration: Do you feel secure in your relationship with your spouse?

_____

_____

_____

_____

_____

_____

_____

Prayer: As you ponder your marriage relationship, what area(s) do you need God's help in feeling secure about your relationship? What prayers do you need?

_____

_____

_____

_____

_____

_____

_____

DAY 18

MARRIAGE IS TRUST

Prior relationships and experiences in your life play a significant role in your ability to trust. Trust in marriage can be compared to having your spouse pack a suitcase for you for an extensive trip. Your suitcase contains your issues, values, and hopes. When you arrive at your destination, you have trust that your spouse has packed those items that you need the most. When you begin to unpack, there are no worries; you have complete trust that your spouse has packed all the necessary items you need for the trip. We have all heard the saying that trust is earned; with trust comes vulnerability. You must be willing to put yourself out there, to expose yourself, to be naked. Emotional nakedness requires total vulnerability, openness, and honesty. When you give someone your heart, you expose the raw part of who you are. You are entrusting that person to take extreme care of your emotions and well-being. You are giving that part of yourself away.

In some cases, trust is not taken seriously. It is used as a pass to get what you want. Trust requires honesty and truthfulness, even if it hurts. Without the Father, true trust can never be obtained. The Bible tells us to trust in no man, because he will fail you (Psalm 146:3). So, what does that mean for you? You must put your trust in Jesus, the author and finisher of your faith. You are not just trusting your spouse; you are trusting in the one who created your spouse. You will always fall short of a promise. It may require an act of forgiveness. You will never be able to fully trust another person without the help of the Father. He is the only one that can give you what you need to be at peace with your spouse. The Bible says that those who trust in themselves are fools, but those who walk in wisdom are kept safe (Proverbs 28:26). This means that the exposed vulnerabilities that you share with your spouse are kept safe in Christ. He protects and guards your heart. He exposes those things that are not right.

So, don't put your trust in your spouse, put your trust in Jesus. He will make things right. He will show you how to trust and believe in the person to whom you have made a vow to spend the rest of your life with him/her. An exercise was performed where a husband had to lead his wife, who was blind folded, through a small obstacle course. She had to listen to his instructions, and in the end, she would be led to a safe place—his arms. That is what your life should look like when you are following Christ in your marriage. Follow your husband's lead as he follows Jesus' lead. Husbands, be led by God and the Holy Spirit as your wife follows you! I know in the day we live in now it is not popular to want to follow someone's lead but in 1 Corinthians 11:1 Paul said, to follow him as he follows Christ. In marriage that same principle applies, you must follow Christ because He should be the lead. When you trust Christ, you can't fail. Even if it seems you are going in the wrong direction, Jesus makes it right. Remember, obedience is better than sacrifice.

Proverbs 3:5-6 says, *"Trust in the LORD with all your heart, and do not lean on your own understanding. In all your ways acknowledge him, and he will make straight your paths"* (ESV).

As you trust God, you can trust your spouse and their decision, because you have put it before the Lord.

Aspiration: In your relationship with your spouse, do you trust him or her? Why or why not?

_____

_____

_____

_____

_____

_____

_____

Prayer: In what area(s) do you need to ask God to help you as it relates to trust in your marriage?

_____

_____

_____

_____

_____

_____

_____

DAY 19

MARRIAGE IS GRACE

Grace is mercy, an allowance of time, of a debt to be paid. Grace is favor shown or goodwill. Everyone is shown grace.

You received God's grace through the redemptive decision that was made on Calvary's cross. In marriage, grace is a decision.

You decide whether or not you are going to forgive.

You decide if you are going to let things go.

You decide if you are going to love past the hurt.

You decide if you are going to go through the healing process.

You decide if the debt has been paid.

You decide if you are going to crash through your quitting point.

You decide to love your spouse more than the situation that

caused discord.

In this life, you will inevitably give your spouse a pass. You are two imperfect people trying to make it in an imperfect world. You will never do everything right. You will not always make the right decision. There will always be a storm that you are about to enter, one that you are currently in, or one you are coming out of. Everyone needs grace. At times, it seems that you give more allowances to the people outside of your home than you do to the one you say you love the most. You put him or her on a pedestal and don't give your spouse the grace to make a mistake.

You don't give him or her the grace card. You become stiff- necked because you feel he or she should know better. In this life as you grow together in your relationship, there are gives and takes. There are rights and wrongs. You will make a mistake. They will make a mistake. It is your responsibility to accentuate the positive and allow your spouse to feel your love in every situation or decision that is made. Everyone deserves a pardon, everyone deserves grace. If God can show grace, then you can too!

Romans 11:5-6 says, *"It is the same today, for a few of the people of Israel have remained faithful because of God's grace—his undeserved kindness in choosing them. And since it is through God's kindness, then it is not by their good works. For in that case, God's grace would not be what it really is—free and undeserved"* (NLT).

James 4:6 says, *"But he gives us more grace. That is why scripture says: God opposes the proud but shows favor to the humble"* (NIV).

If God's grace is free and undeserved, then who are you to not give that same level of kindness to the one you pledged your allegiance to?

Aspiration: Do you give your spouse the grace that he or she should be given?

_____

_____

_____

_____

_____

_____

_____

Prayer: How would you like for God to change you as it relates to grace and your spouse?

_____

_____

_____

M. ANN WEST

_____

_____

_____

_____

DAY 20

MARRIAGE IS PEACE

In the world, there is an atmosphere of fear and hostility. This change causes you to have a diminished sense of peace. Violence has caused havoc on our society. The news is riddled with daily stories of calamity and unrest. Where is the peace? For many years we were a military family. As my husband and I look back on that season of our lives, we thank God that our tour of duty occurred during a peaceful time throughout our travel and his service career. This lack of peace in the world should be a force that drives us to strive to have peace in our homes. What better place to be but in a place where peace and harmony reign!

Peace in your marriage is essential. When you are at peace with your spouse it creates a safe environment.

Peace in your marriage is the bonding agent that allows you

to enjoy one another and look forward to growing old together.

Peace in your marriage creates an atmosphere of harmony.

Peace in your marriage gives you a sense of security.

Peace in your marriage frees your mind and allows you to hear from God.

Peace in your marriage brings you comfort.

Peace in your marriage allows you to sit quietly and gaze into the face of your spouse, and without a word you know their thoughts.

Peace in your marriage fills your heart with the love of the Lord and an appreciation for the gift that God has given you in your spouse.

Peace in your marriage gives you peace of mind in knowing that you are in the right place, doing life with the right person, with whom you have been blessed to be with.

Peace in your marriage is heaven on earth.

Peace in your marriage is what you receive when you trust and believe in the risen Savior.

2 Thessalonians 3:16 says, *"Now the Lord of peace himself give you peace at all times in all ways. The Lord be with you all"* (ASV).

As you look around and see how society handles marriage, you can instinctively be grateful in knowing that your

Savior is the author of peace, therefore you inherit His DNA of peace.

Aspiration: What contributes to your peace as a married couple?

_____

_____

_____

_____

_____

_____

_____

Prayer: As you experience life as a married couple, what is your ultimate prayer for your home as it relates to peace in your home?

_____

_____

_____

_____

_____

_____

_____

M. ANN WEST

DAY 21

MARRIAGE IS A DECISION

You have the choice of who you want to spend the rest of your life with. You also are able to decide if he or she is a good fit for you. Do you both possess the same values and belief system? There are many questions that you may ask before you decide to say, "I do." Every four years as a citizen of the nation, you get to decide who the president of the United States will be. There are many factors to take into account when you decide for whom you are going to vote. Just like politics, our decision on a spouse is based on a variety of options. The difference is once the choice is made you don't get to choose a new spouse every four years. The commitment of marriage is much greater; it is for a life time. Does he or she seem to have the same beliefs as you do? Can he or she be trusted? Can you follow and respect him as your leader?

When you make the decision to marry someone, the vows

you recite to one another is a legal lifelong contract and pledge to one another. You must make a decision to honor your covenant with God. Your love for Christ should be the foundation of your love for your spouse. The decision should be definitive! In society and throughout the world, marriage is not sacred. Marriage is not as important as it used to be. Couples are deciding that it's not that important. Living with one another is comparable to being married. Many of today's couples who choose to live together and not marry are part of a generational curse. They are only doing what their parents did or other family or friends. They don't see the value in a lifelong committed relationship with one person. There are benefits in a covenantal relationship. Jesus is the answer. Without Him your relationship is meaningless.

Many marriages today end in divorce. In a covenant marriage where Jesus is Lord, divorce is not an option. Divorce is not a choice. That is not the decision that we make. It is imperative that you let the Holy Spirit be your guide in your relationship with one another. There is nothing in your relationship that God can't heal. Are you willing to go through it? Are you willing to make the decision that the Lord is the keeper of your relationship? Will you honor God and the agreement that you made with your spouse? One of our former pastors used to say often, "it is a cinch by the inch, but hard by the yard." Daily you take the journey of marriage together with your spouse. When you wake up in the morning, you thank God for another day of life and that you get to do it with the person to whom you said, "I do!"

Hebrews 11:6 says, *"But without faith it is impossible to please him: for he that cometh to God must believe that he is, and that he is a rewarder of them that diligently seek him."*

Since your marriage is more than a four-year term, make your decision count. Choose Christ, choose faith, and choose to seek Him! Choose to love, honor, and respect the person with whom you made a holy covenant.

Aspiration: What decisions have you made concerning your marriage?

_____

_____

_____

_____

_____

_____

Prayer: As you seek to honor your decision and commitment to your marriage, what are you asking God to do for you and your spouse?

_____

_____

_____

_____

_____

_____

_____

FINAL WORDS.....

Marriage is not letting Satan have a foothold in your relationship with one another. So often we allow Satan to enter into our relationship with our spouse. It is at times so subtle that you don't realize it until it is too late, or you may never come to the realization that the enemy is at work to keep you at odds with one another. He knows that there is power in your relationship so he wants to destroy it at all cost. The enemy is the inner me. Your inner self (the heart, your mind) can cause you to believe what you see instead of what you know to be true. The institution of marriage is God's original plan. It is His design. It is His blueprint for how you should live, how you should love, and how you should travel through this life. You are more than a conqueror! You are a victor! You are a winner! With Christ, you can't lose! Though your experience will be unique in many ways, it is your path; it is your story and your journey. God has a plan and the plan requires you and your spouse to be totally dependent on Him. When you fix your eyes on Jesus, you will be successful in sharing a lifetime of hopes and dreams with the person that is a great fit for you; your spouse. Just like the 60th anniversary couple, you will be battled tested, and you will be a living, breathing testimony to show what the power of God, His Word, and His covenant will do. As you continue to grow and understand your spouse, may you lift up a standard of Christian living so that your marriage becomes a taste of heaven on earth and a replica of the love of Christ, who demonstrated the ultimate love sacrifice for you!

Be Blessed!

Marriage is .....

ABOUT THE AUTHOR

M. Ann West is a retired educator, conference and retreat speaker. She is passionate about seeing marriages succeed. She has been married to Wink West for 36 years. The couple have two adult sons, Shawn and Sherrod. They attend Journey Church in Strasburg, PA.

Together they have created a non-profit organization called G.E.M (Growing Every Mind), where they host events for the betterment of families. They are the facilitators of the Marriage Enrichment Ministry. This ministry provides couples with the tools needed for practical living and enhancement of the principals of marriage. In addition to the Marriage Enrichment Ministry, Ann also is the events coordinator for Journey Church.

She is also a part of the Women's Ministry team and serves alongside many other ministries. God has gifted her for a life style of serving. She is blessed to be able to use her hands and feet for the kingdom.

M. ANN WEST

MARRIAGE IS...

www.ingramcontent.com/pod-product-compliance
Lightning Source LLC
Chambersburg PA
CBHW072205090426
42740CB00012B/2399